Flowers

an
Adult Coloring Book

Thank you for choosing our coloring books!

We really hope they will bring you as much enjoyment as they brought us as we created them for you.
Please share your creations on our facebook page http://youcanteatlove.com

Copyright 2021 Joy & Elephants
All rights reserved
No part of this book may be reproduced or transmitted in any form, by any means, electronic or mechanical, including photocopy, without permission in writing from the publisher, except in the case of brief quotations embodied in critical articles and reviews.

Flowers

http://youcanteatlove.com

Printed in Great Britain
by Amazon